Praise for *Wag, Live, Love:*

"*Wag, Live, Love* is a book that works on many levels. The Type A's among us can flourish with Jenks' expertise in helping people achieve their goals; dog lovers will appreciate Magellan's and Tasja's charming way of understanding the world; and anyone with a heart will delight in the pictures of these magnificent Samoyeds. I rate it a full five paws!"
—*Ann Butler,*
Durango Herald,
Durango, Colorado

"Read *Wag, Live, Love* and you will feel happier. Practice the lessons in the book and you will be happier. Enough said!"
—*Jonathan Colton,*
Consultant, Lecturer, and
Fan of Positive Thinking,
New York, NY

"As a horse, dog and cat owner, I have always found animals to be a source of great learning. What Ginger has achieved in this delightful book is to make it possible for each of us to connect on a daily basis with a more positive, more caring, and more humorous way of life. To rephrase an old advertising slogan—a chapter a day will help you work, rest, and play!"
—*Richard Bentley,*
Director, Results Coaching Systems Europe
Cullompton, UK

"This is a gem of a book. It will make you smile, think, laugh, maybe even cry, as you are reminded of what is important in life. Ginger Jenks loves her dogs as she loves life in all its aspects, and through their eyes we get to discover and understand ourselves better—and like ourselves more."
—*Soren Holm,*
Professional Certified Coach,
Stockholm, Sweden

"I felt a renewed sense of purpose and contentment after reading *Wag, Live, Love.* It reminded me of the joy that pets bring to our lives and the lessons they teach, if we will but listen and observe. During a career of working in our court system, I have often observed human behavior that is less than noble. This book is a valuable and enjoyable way to reconnect with what is best in us."
—*The Honorable Susan L. Fowler,*
Chittenden County Probate Judge,
Burlington, VT

Wag, Live, Love

What Dogs Teach Us About Happiness and Life

Tasja and Magellan
with Ginger Jenks, MCC

Agile Holiday
PRESS
Durango, Colorado

First published by AuthorHouse under the title *I Bark Because I Do.*

Illustrations by Martha Lageschulte
Cover photograph by James Cammack

Published by
Agile Holiday Press
Durango, Colorado

www.AgileHoliday.com

ISBN: 978-0-9830046-0-8
LCCN: 2010915981

For information on Wag, Live, Love programs and keynotes, please call 970-259-4847, or email ginger@magellangj.com.

This book is printed on acid-free paper.

Printed in the United States of America

To all the Good Dogs, and the good people who love them.

Acknowledgements

I AM GRATEFUL TO SO MANY people who helped make this book happen. To my many friends, clients, and Building Blocks newsletter readers, who kept after me to write a book. To the people who read drafts of "I Bark" and told me it must be published. To my parents, who gave me my best friend when I was just a year old, and who helped me to see animals as teachers. To my coaches, who provided sage advice, gentle encouragement, and the occasional kick in the butt. To Richard Strozzi-Heckler, for writing the perfect Foreword for *Wag, Live, Love.*

Special thanks to my talented friend James Cammack, whose artistry resurrected my amateur snapshots for the pages of "I Bark," and whose photograph graces the cover of this book. And to my friend Martha Lageschulte, whose wonderful illustrations help bring the stories to life. My friend Karen Thomas designed the cover and template for the stories, adding her special touch to bringing all of the elements together. My editor, J. I. Kleinberg, I thank for dotting my i's and crossing my t's. Pete Masterson, I thank for pulling the package all together for me.

And, of course, I must acknowledge Tasja and Magellan, and all the dogs of my life, whose lives have inspired me in so many ways.

Contents

Foreword

MILLENNIUMS AGO IN A GRASSY swale on a darkening plain a woman gathering roots finds a howling litter of wild puppies in a small den. She folds them into her furs and brings them to her family and they are raised and bred by her clan. On long winter evenings they huddle with the humans and become a source of heat for them; they stand as sentries with bared teeth warning of intruders; they become hunting partners and companions and guardians of the children; they herd cattle and sheep; they pull sleds and transport select objects. They are memorialized in paintings on cave walls and drawn on drumheads and cloaks and their fangs and claws fashioned into weapons. Their fur and bones are worn and displayed as art and the most esteemed among them are adorned with colored ribbons and woven leather, distinguishing their myth of power and beauty. Throughout generations an intimate and sacred relationship has been cultivated between our ancestors and Canis familiaris.

Over time our relationship with dogs has developed and evolved through many forms, both utilitarian and exotic. Currently dogs are used therapeutically in convalescent and nursing homes, as companions for the elderly, the alone and the halt, guide dogs for the blind, guard dogs, and in schools. There is research indicating that having a dog companion produces quicker recovery from illness or surgery, that dogs generate positive moods in people, and that children raised with dogs have stronger immune systems in later life.

Walking through an average office space today it's not uncommon to see framed photos of people's dogs alongside photos of their spouses, children, and grandchildren. Ginger Jenks is one of these people. Ginger is a successful Executive Coach and before that she was a successful executive; she's also a world-class skier and an avid outdoorswoman. Her centers of gravity, however, are her Samoyeds, who are also agility and conformation champions, and successful on a national level. In the decade-plus that I've known Ginger I can't remember a conversation with her when one of her "Sammies" has not been mentioned with the corresponding lift in energy and affection in her voice.

This relationship is not simply sentimental. Ginger is an exceptional dog trainer and an astute observer of not only her Samoyeds, but of all dogs, as well as us two-leggeds. This power of observation is what makes her a Master Coach and allows her to put into words the wisdom that we can learn from our canine friends. These are the eyes of deep love and patient discipline.

This is a common sense, straightforward book about how to live a balanced, sane, and happy life. It will bring a head-nodding affirmation from dog owners and it has something important to say to everyone. It is funny, it is wise, and it makes you a better observer of yourself and the world. Let it touch your funny bone as well as your soul.

Richard Strozzi-Heckler, PhD
Author of *The Leadership Dojo*
and *The Anatomy of Change*
www.strozziinstitute.com

Introduction

Tasja and Magellan are the storytellers in *Wag, Live, Love,* and they are also the main characters. While the stories are from these two particular dogs' lives, they are also the stories of all of our dogs. My role has been to witness, record, and expand their stories.

Tasja and Magellan are Samoyeds, a beautiful breed named after the Samoyede Eskimo people. Samoyeds are white, fluffy, strong, gentle, playful, loving dogs. Originally bred to herd reindeer, pull sleds, and keep their humans warm during arctic nights, Samoyeds are incredible beings, with much to teach about life. While this is true of many dogs, this book offers the perspective of "The Sammy Way."

In my career as an Executive Coach, I have coached hundreds of people, from CEOs to dog agility competitors. The one thing all of these clients have in common is that they are on a quest for more happiness. Some wish to accomplish great business feats, some want more balance in their lives, and some want to achieve a particular goal. But all of those things are simply expressions of what that person believes will make him or her happier.

What I have noticed in my life with Samoyeds, as a companion and as a competitor, is that dogs offer really insightful lessons on how to live a happier life. This book is my distillation of some of those lessons into bite-size stories. Stories are often the most powerful way to make learning memorable. Each story is followed by three "Thoughtful Paws," which are designed to anchor and expand the wisdom in the story from my perspective as a professional coach.

Dogs are masters at living in the present moment. They are optimists. They love and forgive in ways that humans can't fathom. They have wisdom. In this era of more and more restrictions on dogs and their humans, it is important to remember the value dogs add to our lives. Dogs expand our humanity. They help us to connect with each other.

I hope you'll share this book with friends and your children, and use the stories as a way to talk about such things as Sharing, Forgiveness, Grief, Friends, and Joy. I hope it will help many people learn what a gift animals can be in our lives, and how they teach us respect for life.

Try reading one story each day. Think about how you might practice some of the concepts in your life. Maybe you want to play more, or try something new. While the stories are meant to entertain, they are also intended to provoke thought and emotion. Most importantly, they offer simple pathways for living more happily.

Tasja and Magellan were born in Massachusetts. They weren't show dogs, but they sure did show me a lot! They traveled all over the United States with me in 1997, and then settled with me in our new home in Colorado. My life has been much richer because of their wonderful companionship. They have made me a better person, and a happier person—no doubt about it.

There is an oft-quoted saying that's one of my favorites: "May I always be the person my dog thinks I am." Imagine what the world would be like if we could all be that person!

Ginger Jenks, Master Certified Coach
Durango, Colorado
January, 2010

The author with Tasja and Magellan.

Coming Home

I came Home today! I didn't know it was Home until tonight. I have a human named Ginger, who's just great. She pets me, and feeds me, and took me for a walk, and gave me a bunch of toys. At first I thought this was just an adventure, but tonight, as I'm snuggled up in my new bed with my stuffed Bunny, I know it's Home.

I'm only 9 weeks old, so I don't know a whole lot yet, but this is what I think Home is:

1. It's where you belong. You're welcome, and a part of everything.
2. You're safe at Home.
3. You get to be comfortable. Do stuff. Make it your own. I've already started making it my own by peeing on a few things. Puppies do that. Ginger says I'll learn quickly to go outside, and I will. I want to please!
4. You have family. Even though my Samoyed mom and brothers and sisters aren't here, I can tell that Ginger is going to be my family. My stuffed bunny and ducky aren't really family, but I like having them around, anyway.

It was a little scary at first. I'd never been in a car before, and we drove all the way from Plymouth to Ashland, Massachusetts. Even though I am from Plymouth, I am not a Pilgrim. I am Magellan. Ginger Says Magellan was an explorer. I plan to explore everything!

There is a nice, big, grassy yard here. I think it will be good to dig in. It's been a pretty Big Day.

THOUGHTFUL PAWS

🐾 *How do you feel when you come Home? Does your place feel safe, comfortable, loving, and welcoming? How might you make it more so?*

🐾 *Home is not always a place. It is also a state of mind. With whom do you feel at Home? Taking care of these relationships is one of the best investments of time and heart that you can make.*

🐾 *How adept are you at making others feel at Home? Developing your capacity for this will expand the quality and depth of your relationships. We're all at our best and most resourceful when we feel safe, comfortable, loved, and welcomed.*

Magellan as a puppy, delighted with his new home.

Love Unlimited

I've been Home for almost four months now, and I think I'm doing really well, if I do say so myself. There were a few rough spots, like when I took the contact lens case out of Ginger's gym bag and ate it (yum… salty!), or cleared three shrubs out of the yard. But I helped Ginger practice Forgiveness, and I'm learning what are Good Ideas, and what are Bad Ideas.

But then, TODAY! Today, Ginger brought home a little girlfriend for me! She is, without question, the best thing Ginger has EVER brought me! Tasja is a Samoyed puppy, like me. Only she's about a fifth of the size of me. I am so excited, I can just about stand it. I have been playing with her all day. I can fit her whole head in my mouth. She's a little bit wet from that.

My human, Ginger, (*my* human) has been paying quite a bit of attention to this Tasja puppy. I was a little concerned at first—would there be enough love left for me? And if I play with Tasja all the time, will I have enough love for Ginger, too?

Here's what I've decided. Love is unlimited. It seemed crazy at first, because, for instance, the food in my bowl is not unlimited. But Ginger seems to be able to love me, and love Tasja, too. There's plenty! And I don't seem to run out of love at all. I have enough for Tasja, Ginger, and anybody else who happens to come over. I can give as much as I want. Kind of like boy dogs peeing on trees. There's always more available!

THOUGHTFUL PAWS

🐾 *Sometimes, it's easy for humans to feel that love is a limited thing. That we have only so much capacity for friends, family, community, and a partner. It can be an amazing shift to realize that we have as much love to offer (and often to receive, as well) as we want. There is no limit to how much we can love, in depth or breadth.*

🐾 *When we have a relationship that we cherish, fear can creep in when someone else enters the picture, getting some of the loving attention that we so treasure. We can stay in a loving and kind place by remembering that this does not mean that there will be less for us.*

🐾 *Dogs are such wonderful examples of loving abundance. They give you their whole heart, every day, for all of their lives. We humans can be a bit more guarded. Imagine what it would be like to give your whole heart, every day, for the rest of your life.*

Imagine what it would be like to give your whole heart, every day, for the rest of your life.

LOVE UNLIMITED

Moderation Might be Good

When I was just an 8-week old puppy, Ginger had a big barbecue party. Everybody made a fuss over me, and gave me turkey, and ham, and all kinds of good things. Boy oh boy! I could hardly walk up the steps after the feast. I think I ate about as much food as I weighed! I wasn't feeling all that well… still…. I could maybe eat a bit more.

After everyone left, I patrolled the house to see what goodies might have been left unattended. In the den, there was a big bowl of M&M'S® on the coffee table. Just my height! It must have been left for *me!*

I'd never had candy before. M&M'S are YUMMY! But chocolate is a bad idea for any dog, it turns out. Especially for a puppy who had already eaten way too much "people" food.

Fortunately, the M&M'S didn't stay in my tummy for too long. Ginger caught me with my face in the bowl and said, "NO!" I got scared and threw up on the rug. Oops. Too much of a good thing.

I never really did learn that lesson very well… it's hard not to want more and more of a good thing. But too much of anything can hurt you. I still like M&M'S, though. Just a few, please!

THOUGHTFUL PAWS

🐾 *Moderation is such a good idea… in theory. How skilled are you in moderating such things as eating, spending, and sleeping? What short and long term benefits would accrue with even a 10% improvement?*

🐾 *In our desire to show appreciation for another being, be it a dog or a human, we can sometimes overdo it, with such things as food or gifts. Consider other ways to show appreciation, such as being present, or conversation.*

🐾 *Is a lack of moderation causing negative consequences in any area of your life? What would it take to turn that around?*

Tasja tuckered out after her first party.

MODERATION MIGHT BE GOOD

I Bark Because I Do

I bark because I do. Bark, bark, bark, bark, bark! Telling me, "No Bark!" isn't useful….I am the way I am, and there's some things you just have to accept in others. Bark! Bark! I like to bark. I bark when I'm happy, I bark when I'm scared, I bark when I want something, and I bark for no reason at all. I bark because I do. So there!

Ginger put a "no bark" collar on me once. Foul! Fortunately, I got Tasja to chew it off me. Ginger didn't seem too pleased about this… she said something about "There goes $150…." She said I had to learn to be a good neighbor. Of course I want to be a good neighbor. I just don't understand what barking has to do with that.

Sometimes Ginger squirts me with a water gun when I bark… I duck. It's a good game! I also like to get a drink from it. I try to stop barking when Ginger asks me to, but that is really hard. Sometimes, a couple still slip out. Hopefully my many excellent qualities outweigh this one little fault. Please love me as I am. I promise to do the same for you.

Bark! Bark! I love to bark. It's part of being Magellan. Joy to the world! Bark! Bark!

THOUGHTFUL PAWS

* Some things can change in others, some things can't. Be willing to accept the things you can't change, if you value the other person (or dog). Habits or character traits are sometimes just the way people are.

* A dog's intentions are good. Always. But those intentions can manifest in ways that aren't comprehensible, or desirable, to humans. Remember that the dog's intentions are always good.

* What things about you might drive other people a little crazy? Is it worth modifying your behavior? Is it possible to do so, or are some of those things "just you"?

GINGER JENKS

Magellan pausing for a moment, mid-bark.

Try New Things

I like to try new things. Take food, for example.

    I like lots of weird stuff—carrots, broccoli, and asparagus. People are always surprised by that, but maybe their dogs just never **tried** carrots, broccoli, and asparagus. My philosophy is, give it a try—it might be delicious! But when Ginger gives me something new, I might spit it out first. After all, it might be a pill or something similarly disgusting. One must have limits.

    Our regular life routine is pretty darned good. We go for walks, play with fun toys, have good meals, and go for car rides. That's like the meat and potatoes. Solid and tasty. Trying new things is the **dessert!** Things like riding on a windsurfer on Lake Winnepesaukee in New Hampshire, or hiking in the canyons of Moab, Utah.

    I am an excellent windsurfer! OK, I didn't actually sail the thing on my own, but I rode that board with a lot of style, I'll tell you. And I also rode it while Ginger sailed it. I might occasionally be a little nervous trying something new, but it's still exciting and fun. Ginger says that Samoyeds used to herd reindeer in the arctic. I could do that. Piece of cake.

    Sometimes when I try new things, Ginger is grossed out. Take elk poop, for example—**yum!** She doesn't know what she's missing… hey Magellan, do you want some?

THOUGHTFUL PAWS

🐾 *It's easy to get comfortable in a routine, and bypass trying new things. What are two new things you would like to try this year? Has your life been limited by not trying new things?*

🐾 *What is the best atmosphere for you to try new things? By yourself? With friends? With strangers?*

🐾 *Think of a time when you tried something new and absolutely loved it (at least by the end of the experience). Anchor that into your memory and recall it when next confronted with trying something new.*

Magellan windsurfing on Lake Winnepesaukee, NH.

TRY NEW THINGS

Sharing

Y ou know, I don't think sharing always comes naturally. I have to work at it, and think about it. But I'm always glad when I do share. Not all dogs are good at sharing. Some humans are better at it than others, too.

Sometimes, like when I have some good food, I think, "I want it all for myself! It's so good, and there's not that much of it!" But then, if I give some to Tasja, I see how much she likes me for it. That warm feeling is better than food! OK, maybe *just* as good as food.

When Tasja and I each have a rawhide chewy, sometimes Tasja forgets about sharing and takes my chewy, even though she's got her own. It makes me cry. Then she remembers her manners and gives it back. Sometimes I think she takes my chewy just to see if I'll let her have it. I always will, too. I want her to be happy.

Ginger shares with me a lot. It's great! Steak, cookies, whatever. Share and share alike, I say!

THOUGHTFUL PAWS

🐾 *Sharing is much easier for humans in a mindset of abundance than in one of scarcity. Dogs seem to have naturally generous spirits. What would it take to cultivate a consistently generous spirit in humans, individually and collectively?*

🐾 *All of us, from time to time, struggle with sharing. We might be selective about with whom we share, and how much. Dogs, of course, mostly share time and affection, and do so without reservation. What makes it so much more difficult for us to share without reservation?*

🐾 *What is the best memory you have about sharing? What makes it the best one?*

Sharing a toy, the sofa, and a moment.

SHARING

It's Good to be Queen

It's good to be Queen. My subjects adore me, and I lovingly rule them. Treats are offered to me, which is as it should be. Magellan, my loyal friend and servant, lavishes kisses on my eyes, ears, and mouth. A little to the left, please. That's enough, thank you. No, no, get off my back! I'm the Queen, remember?

Everyone should have the opportunity to feel like a Queen now and then. Like maybe on your birthday! Or maybe just for no reason at all.

People talk about "owning" dogs sometimes. But let me ask you this: "Who is fed breakfast and dinner every day, hugged, played with, presented with wonderful treats like bones, brushed for hours, and gets to sleep most of the day?" It's not my person, I can tell you that. C'est *moi!* Do I ever "scoop poop"? Never. That's human work.

I wonder if people ever treat each other like they were Queen, or if this special treatment is reserved just for dogs? It certainly keeps me in good spirits, and I am very appreciative and loyal.

Yes, I *would* like a cookie! No, I can't come over there and "shake hands" for it. I'm resting comfortably here, and—I am *awfully* cute! Would you please bring the offering over here to me? Thank you *so* much. The Queen is very pleased and grateful!

THOUGHTFUL PAWS

🐾 *When was the last time you got to be Queen? It's good to be Queen! If it's been a while, commit to making it happen at least once a quarter. Do whatever makes you feel that way — a spa day, reading a good book, or going to a baseball game.*

🐾 *Make the effort to surprise the people in your life every now and then with a "Be the Queen" gesture. It can be as simple as cooking a nice meal for someone, or giving them a hand with a chore or project.*

🐾 *This is a great place to practice not Keeping Score. When you make a "Be the Queen" moment happen for someone else, do it without expectation of a return gesture. If you are the recipient of such largesse, simply thank your benefactor graciously and enjoy!*

GINGER JENKS

A Queen needs her beauty rest.

Friends are Better than Cookies

I t's great to have friends. Tasja is my best friend. Ginger is my other best friend.

Friends do things with you, like go for walks, watch TV, play ball, or just take a nap. Friends like you no matter what. Even if I make a mistake, Ginger still likes me. Even if Tasja gets mad at me for a minute, like if I borrow her bone, she still likes me. True friends always forgive each other.

Friends do things for each other. Ginger feeds me and rubs my tummy. And scratches my ears—that's the best! I give Tasja lots of kisses—on her eyes, ears, and mouth! Most of the time she likes it, I think. I sleep next to Ginger's bed. I keep watch over her to make sure nothing bad ever happens. One time, the washing machine in the basement overflowed. I sounded the alert, just like Lassie! Friends look out for each other.

Sometimes friends do tough stuff for you, too. Like take you to the vet. The things friends do together aren't always fun. But just about anything you do is better if you do it with a friend. Friends help each other out.

I'm a good friend. Loyal, trustworthy, kind, thoughtful. I'm lucky I have good friends, too. Cookies are one of my very favorite things in life, but friends are even better than cookies.

THOUGHTFUL PAWS

🐾 Sometimes, we take the blessing of friendship for granted. What action would it take on your part in the next thirty days for your friends to know how much you appreciate them?

🐾 Is there something a friend of yours is going through right now, where you might be able to lessen the burden? Even listening can be a wonderful gift for a friend who is struggling.

🐾 Like any living thing, friendship requires nourishment to thrive. Think how to nourish your most important friendships on a regular basis. Even for those long distance or infrequent contact friendships, nourishment is important. The fact that nourishment requires effort is exactly what makes it so endearing.

GINGER JENKS

Hiking buddies visiting Sedona, AZ.

FRIENDS ARE BETTER THAN COOKIES

Holidays

Holidays are special times. Good food, good company, and sometimes, even presents!

I got some new toys last Christmas—it was ***excellent!*** I got a stuffed dinosaur that squeaks, some rawhide chewies (yum!) and a little stuffed wolf pup that howls. I also got to spend time with a bunch of people who were feeling happy and wanted to give me treats. Bring it on!

Magellan, Ginger, and I visited the "nursing home" quite a bit, back in Massachusetts. The old folks there seemed especially happy to see us when we went around holidays. Some of them said they felt very sad until we arrived to visit. Mimi, one of the ladies who lived there, called us the Christmas Dogs, even when it wasn't Christmas. She said we made her feel like it was Christmas. I liked that. It felt like Christmas to me, too.

I don't know why we can't have holidays every day. I like getting dressed up, and seeing everyone in a good mood. I like spending time with my family and friends. You know what? To me, every day ***is*** a holiday. Why not?

THOUGHTFUL PAWS

🐾 *Every day is a holiday for dogs. Of course, dogs don't have to shop for presents, meet deadlines for holiday cards, or cook big feasts and clean up after them. They just enjoy the good mood and good food. Would that be possible for us?*

🐾 *Humans make a point of getting together "for the holidays." We travel at the same time, compete for our guests' time and attention, and crowd our calendars with too many gatherings in too little time. Why do we need a holiday to make a point of getting together? Dogs celebrate being with us on every occurrence.*

🐾 *Because every day is a holiday for dogs, they don't expect things to be "extra special" on any particular day. People often feel a lot of pressure around the holidays. We create this by expecting things to look and be a certain way. What would happen if we were just open to what happens?*

Tasja and Magellan get into the holiday spirit.

Simple Pleasures are the Best

You know, nothing beats a good skritch! What's a skritch? It's somewhere between a scratch and a rub. I like to have my ears skritched, especially. It makes me groan with happiness…. "Uuuuuuuunnnnnnnnnnnnggggggggggghhhhhhhh!" Go ahead, try it! Skritch your head… now, groan with happiness! Good, huh?

I like to have my belly skritched, too. That's why my nickname is "Gelly Belly." I roll on my back and wave my paws to ask for a belly skritch…. I don't know HOW I could be more clear. Honestly, humans just don't get it sometimes! The simplest of communications. People make things more difficult than they need to be.

The simple pleasures in life are often the best. A good skritch beats even the coolest new toy. A walk in the sunshine beats fancy food. A hug beats going to the groomer, hands down! And taking a nap snuggled up with my favorite person? Why, that can't be beat. It seems like humans have all this Stuff to try and make themselves happy—TVs, cars, skis, boats. I'm glad it is so much easier for me—I just experience the simple pleasures that are already all around me.

You know what's good, too? I like having the top of my butt skritched! Dogs can get away with that. People can't.

THOUGHTFUL PAWS

- *What are your Top 3 Simple Pleasures? Make a commitment to experience all of them more consciously. It's amazing what a little Mindfulness can do.*

- *Think about the things that consume the most time and money in your life. Do they also bring you the most happiness?*

- *If you had to live without all of your "stuff"—TV, car, stereo, skis, etc.—to what degree would your enjoyment of life change? Try it for a week.*

Magellan gets a group hug.

KENDALL GEORGES

Because You See Me, I Am Here

Have you ever been ignored? It bites. Of course, I do my best to not allow that to happen. A cold nose, twinkling eyes, or shoving my head under somebody's hand seems to work pretty well. And if needed, a bark or a "Woo, woo, WOO!" is pretty effective, too. And when someone really *sees* me, it makes me feel just grand. It makes me wag my tail. It makes my heart go thump, thump, THUMP! It's better than a cookie.

Here's what I notice. People respond to dogs so well because we SEE people, acknowledge them, and generally adore them. Goodness, it's not so hard! Yet I see humans walking around Hangdog (silly expression, in my opinion), because they feel invisible to the world. It's a People Game. But games are supposed to be fun, and I think people are sad when they feel ignored or invisible.

Back in Massachusetts, we would visit a nursing home. You should have seen those people light up when I would SEE them! Some even cried, they were so happy. It's good to see and be seen!

I do my best to say, "I See You" to everyone I run into. And the proper response to that is, "I Am Here." And when you see me, I Am Here.

THOUGHTFUL PAWS

🐾 What percentage of the time do you make other people feel fully "seen," or acknowledged, as fellow human beings? Do you have different standards with family, friends, employees, and strangers?

🐾 Recall a time that someone really saw you. How did it make you feel? What about that person's communication made it happen that way?

🐾 Take a day, or a week, and make a conscious effort to practice this way of being with everyone you encounter. Notice how others respond to you, and how you feel, as well. Then embrace this practice into your life.

Tasja with her "Mona Lisa" smile, snuggled against Magellan.

BECAUSE YOU SEE ME, I AM HERE

Gratitude, Every Day

Being grateful means being happy for what you have. Like a warm bed, food to eat, cookies and bones, hugs from your person, dog pals to play with, let's not forget about toys, dirt to dig in, trees to lift your leg on, birds/bunnies/cats to chase, doorbells to bark at, goodness! The list goes on and on.

As a dog, I don't think much about what else I want… I never think, "Oh, if only I had a NEW toy, the latest model of the squeaky ducky, life would be so much better!" There's so much to appreciate right in front of me. Now, I'm not saying that I don't covet what's on someone else's dinner table occasionally, but I'm still grateful for whatever I get.

I go for a walk every single day. I am always grateful for my walks. I love the exercise, the exciting smells, fresh air, and companionship. We often run into other people and dogs, and that's a wonderful bonus.

As a matter of fact, I am so grateful for my good life that I never even THINK about longing for a Caribbean vacation, or winning the Lottery! It's interesting, people seem to always be talking about what **else** they want. They miss out on being grateful for what's right in front of them, today. Not me. Gratitude, every day. All the time. Keeps me very, very happy.

THOUGHTFUL PAWS

🐾 *Dogs are very easy to please. They are grateful to be alive. Humans have to practice gratitude. Too often, humans look at what they don't have, instead of what they do. A great practice upon waking in the morning, and retiring at night, is to think of ten different things for which you are grateful.*

🐾 *When things go well for people, there can be a temptation to say, "I earned it." While that may be so, it's also a great opportunity to be in gratitude, for all the unknown and uncontrollable factors that went your way.*

🐾 *Dogs are grateful for even the most simple, basic things in their lives—a pat on the head, a breakfast of kibble, or a morning walk. Humans often become blind to all the blessings available to them every day, every hour. Opening awareness to this abundance on a daily basis increases personal happiness dramatically.*

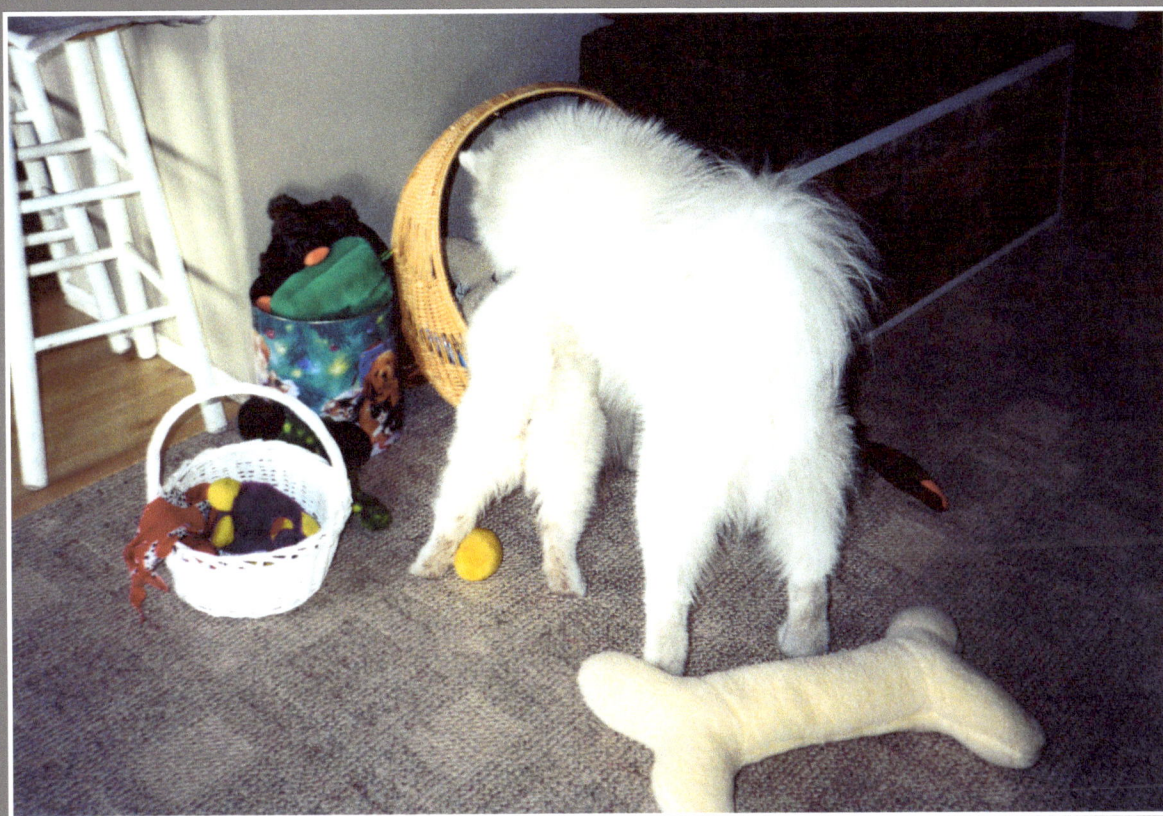

Appreciating the abundance in their lives, "shopping" in the toy basket.

Living Takes Time

Humans seem to be in such a hurry, almost all of the time. I'm in a hurry really only three times:

1. When it's time to eat, and my dinner bowl is in the air, instead of on the floor!
2. When the doorbell rings, and the door's not open yet.
3. When I've been inside too long, and need to go out for a "bio break."

But people, they seem to be in a rush from the moment they get up to when they fall asleep. I could (almost) get exhausted just watching Ginger doing this. (By the way, Ginger is a funny name for a person, isn't it? I know lots of dogs named Ginger. It'd be like naming a dog David.) I try to get her to slow down by presenting my tummy for scratching, or by sniffing things on our walk, or by bringing a toy for us to play with. Living takes time! You have to take time to live.

We dogs don't live as long as humans, not at all! Maybe ten years, fourteen if we're lucky. Yet we take time to live every day. The important things are being loving, playing, seeing the world with wonderment, and enjoying morning sunshine, a cold nip in the air or a warm breeze. This is a sweet life! In the rush and complexity, don't bury the sweetness. Bury your bones, but never life's sweetness.

THOUGHTFUL PAWS

* *When you're in a big hurry, are you more, or less, likely to be the person you want to be with others?*

* *What very important things may have been overlooked in your life over the past few years, while being "really busy"?*

* *What brings you joy? How often do you allow yourself to actually stop, and revel in that joy? What might make it easier to do so?*

Magellan taking time to smell the flowers.

LIVING TAKES TIME

Forgiveness is a Gift

Forgiving someone feels good! I can tell that it feels even better for whomever I'm forgiving. What a nice gift.

I remember once when Ginger stepped on me by accident, and the times she had to give me shots. I cried because it hurt at the time. She was so sorry, though! I immediately let her know that it was OK, that I forgave her. Of course! Why would I want to stay mad at my friend, somebody I love? That just makes things worse. Forgiving makes things better, right away.

It hurts to have somebody stay mad at you when you've made a mistake, like throwing up on the carpet. When you make a mistake, it's not like you can take it back, for crying out loud. Let's get over it. It's way better to have somebody hope your upset tummy is feeling better, and stroke your head. Sometimes I get mad at Magellan, just for a minute, because he's trying to eat my food or jumping on me (**boys!—can't live with 'em, can't live without 'em**). I've even growled at him when he made me really mad. But he looks so crushed, I immediately feel sorry, and let him know. He forgives me instantly. What a pal.

The next time you're really mad at somebody (even when you know you're right), try forgiving them right away. Do it in your heart—that's the most important place.

THOUGHTFUL PAWS

🐾 *Dogs have an amazing ability to forgive, instantly. Think how different life would be if people were able to let things go that quickly, rather than harboring grudges.*

🐾 *Are there people who have not forgiven you for a past mistake? What effect has that had on your relationship?*

🐾 *Think about a time when you had difficulty in forgiving someone. What was the barrier in letting it go?*

GINGER JENKS

Forgiving makes things better, right away.

Play

Have you played enough today? Play is the juice of life! I like to play fetch, wrestle with Tasja, dig in the snow, play hide and seek… any old game! Sometimes when I haven't felt well I didn't feel like playing. What dreary days those were! It also stinks if nobody wants to play with you. That doesn't happen too often for me, thank goodness. But I can also amuse myself pretty well, when I have to. I can throw the ball to myself, and once I had a Big Time barking at myself in the mirror (well, I didn't know it was me in the mirror at first, OK?!)

You can tell people who don't play enough—B-O-R-I-N-G!! Can you imagine a life without play? I can't. I could give lessons in how to play your life away… I'm an excellent player! It's probably why I've lived so long. That's what I tell people who say, "Magellan, what's your secret for a long, happy life?" Play, play, play, play. Eat, too! At every opportunity!

THOUGHTFUL PAWS

* *What does it take for you to play? An invitation? Time? When was the last time that you initiated play?*

* *Dogs invite us to play all the time. Do you invite other people to play with you? Does it matter if you know them well, or do you initiate play with anyone?*

* *Play opportunities abound! Make a practice of finding at least one opportunity a day for a little play. Dogs and kids make this easy; but look for opportunities to play with other adults. Notice what happens in terms of creativity, trust, and relaxation.*

Arctic dog with coolness.

P L A Y

Life is an Adventure!

Six months ago, we went for a ride in the car. Ginger had loaded our Ford Explorer (Ginger calls it the Fancy Dog Crate) with a bunch of stuff, so Magellan and I knew it might be a vacation car ride or something. But now the Explorer feels like Home.

Ginger says this house in Durango, Colorado, is our new Home. We have traveled thousands of miles, all over the U.S. Ginger calls it "The Sabbatical." I think that's a fancy name for "Road Trip." My favorite stops were the Grand Canyon, and Arches National Park. Hundreds of new friends came up to meet us! Ginger's friend Jack came with us some of the way, but he was a little cranky, so we decided to stay happy and go on without Jack. Life is an Adventure!

We dogs like routine, but we're also very adaptable. Ginger calls that a Paradox. As long as Magellan and Ginger are with me, that's enough routine for me. Adventures are fun and exciting, and they can be scary, too. Like when I got sick in Utah, and we had to find an emergency vet. But we also had some of the very best times in our life, like when we were at Island in the Sky in Canyonlands National Park in Utah. Wow.

I don't know what it will be like in this new Home. Magellan (the dog Explorer!) and I are checking everything out. We've been up in the mountains, and that sure is nice. It's getting hard for me to remember our home back in Boston. There's so much new to see here! The world is a much bigger place than I ever thought. I can tell that Ginger is a little nervous about our new life, sometimes. She'll figure it out. Life is an Adventure!

THOUGHTFUL PAWS

🐾 *Adventure means different things to different people. For some, it might be mountain climbing in the Himalayas, while for others it might be trying a new restaurant. The important thing to remember is that there is value in the adventure itself, regardless of the result. Explore!*

🐾 *Adventure does not typically equal comfort. Expect there to be some bumps and discomfort in any adventure you embark upon. Good stories for later!*

🐾 *Dogs look at many things as an adventure—a hike, a car ride, staying in a hotel room. They are excited and interested in something new. We humans can get so busy and stressed that we overlook the adventure aspect that is present in many of the things we get to do, such as a business trip. How might you ignite your adventure awareness?*

Hiking up Missionary Ridge in Durango, CO.

LIFE IS AN ADVENTURE.

Patience Wins the Day

You know how sometimes you want something, and you want it *now?* Sometimes you don't get what you want, though, no matter how loud you bark, or how charming you are, or how many cool tricks you do. This can lead to major frustration.

Patience is the ticket. I've learned that if I'm patient, I often get what I want. I try different things, and I'm patient. If I don't succeed, I don't get very discouraged—I'm patient. I try, and try again. Does it always work? No, it doesn't. But the odds go way up!

Begging at the dinner table is pretty much a waste of time. But begging at the *end* of dinner, now that's a different story. The humans are going to be scraping the plates anyway, their tummies are full, and there's generally a few tasty tidbits left on the plate. And they don't feel like they're "feeding me at the table." Please.

Once, we were watching a Durango Snowdown canine fashion show in the parking lot of McDonald's. I love McDonald's, don't you? There was a man there, and I could just tell he had a bunch of delicious, fresh food in his McDonald's bag. I could have just grabbed it, but I didn't. Not me.

I smiled at him, barked at him once, sat up, smiled some more, and wagged my tail. Over and over. Again and again. Finally, after about 10 minutes, he yelled across the parking lot to his 12-year-old daughter, "Honey, can I give the dog your hamburger?" And that's just what he did! Patience wins the day.

THOUGHTFUL PAWS

* *Dogs are resilient. How resilient are you? If you're told no, do you take it personally, or do you patiently figure out how to try again?*

* *Consider a time when patience is difficult… say, waiting in traffic when you're going to be late. Are you able to take it in stride, or are you ready to explode? Given that neither will influence the traffic, and only one will help your peace of mind, cultivating the practice of patience might be handy.*

* *Sometimes, patience is about knowing when the time is right, and being ready to move when that time comes. How skilled are you at being patient enough to wait, and aware enough to pounce?*

GINGER JENKS

"I can wait…"

See the World as a Friendly Place

You know what I really like? Going for walks and car rides! There are so many new things to discover. People miss a lot when they don't stop to smell the roses—or the fire hydrant.

It's really fun when we go for a walk down Main Avenue in downtown Durango. I want to meet all the people and dogs! I smile, wag my tail, and say, "Hi! I'm Tasja! Want to be friends?" Pretty much everybody responds well to that invitation. Sometimes you run into a cranky person or dog, but I figure it must just be their Bad Day.

I wonder why humans aren't as friendly toward each other as we dogs are to everybody. I see tons of humans downtown that NEVER run up to each other to introduce themselves. (And sniff each other? Forget about it! Never happens.)

I remember this one man I met… Not only were people not speaking to him, they were actually walking away from him. He was talking to himself, and he had a lot of really interesting smells. I went right up to him to introduce myself, and Magellan did, too. This man was so beautiful! His face lit up, and he knelt down to pet us. He told Ginger what wonderful dogs we were. I liked him, too. He had tears in his eyes as he thanked us for making his day. Heck, it was easy! I heard people whisper that he was "homeless," and "a street person." I don't know what those things mean.

THOUGHTFUL PAWS

🐾 *Do you tend to see the world as a friendly place? Are strangers friends you just haven't met, or are you cautious, or even suspicious? Consider how this colors your experience every day.*

🐾 *Are you someone who says "hello" to people you don't know? How do others react when you do?*

🐾 *What opportunities close down when you see the world as an unfriendly place? Are you one way in one environment (like your home town) and another way in a different place?*

Magellan and Nia, a Bernese Mountain Dog puppy, are friends who just met.

Show Your Affection

We dogs are especially good at being affectionate. We offer doggy kisses, we cuddle, we snuggle, and we love to be petted, hugged and cuddled back.

I especially like to kiss people on the lips. They try to offer me their cheek, but nothing but lips will do for me! I wait for just the right moment, when someone isn't expecting it, then plant a big wet one on 'em! Ginger's friend Michael was talking baby talk to me this one time… of course that made me give him a kiss! He said, "Yuck," which I'm sure is a human way of saying, "Thanks, Magellan!"

Dogs never withhold love. People sometimes pretend they don't like each other, to get what they want, or to punish somebody—I don't know, stupid stuff, if you ask me. I wish I could spend more time with everybody I love. I try to show my affection in lots of ways. I follow Ginger around, bark at her when she comes home, lick her, put my head on her knee, and sleep on the floor right next to her bed. I give Tasja lots of kisses, play with her, and share my toys with her.

How about you? Have you been showing your affection enough? Don't be afraid. Don't be shy. Don't withhold. Love, love, show your love! Quick! Do it now! It feels great!

THOUGHTFUL PAWS

🐾 *One of the wonderful things about dogs is that most people immediately feel they have permission to show open affection to a dog, with touch, and with words. All of us have people that we care about. What a difference it would make in our lives if we were to express our affection more frequently, more openly, and more enthusiastically!*

🐾 *In the quest to be "cool," professional, or controlling, humans sometimes withhold their affection. To use something sweet like affection as a weapon is just wrong. Can you imagine a dog withholding its love? They aren't even capable of that.*

🐾 *Fear of rejection can be a barrier to humans showing their affection. Dogs don't seem to experience this same fear, nor do they seem very hurt if their offering of affection is rejected. What would it be like for you to offer affection so fearlessly?*

Tasja enjoys a kiss on the ear from Magellan.

S H O W   Y O U R   A F F E C T I O N

A Winning Smile

A winning smile can take you a long way in life. I have a beautiful smile! I smile at people, wave my luxurious tail like a flag, and life just seems to flow nicely—good things come my way.

Think about it. Smiles are way too rare. You run into people who look so serious—sad, worried, or mad. It makes you want to get away from them. A winning smile is an easy way to stand out—there's not much competition! Just about everybody smiles back at me, too. Try it.

Sometimes Ginger and I don't see eye to eye about what needs doing when. There are times when I really think a walk is in order, or a book needs eating. I remember eating something called a "rare" (it tasted well done to me!) music history book, and that had Ginger definitely ***not*** smiling. I think we'd even have to call her behavior downright cranky. But I just kept smiling, and sure enough, after a while Ginger smiled, too. All is forgiven.

We Samoyeds are lucky. We're born with winning smiles—it's actually called "the Sammy Smile." You might have to work at it. But I guarantee you'll get great results—a tummy rub, a cookie, some steak—your heart's desire! Take it from me—the Smile Queen!

THOUGHTFUL PAWS

🐾 *When something goes awry, our first impulse is often anger, fear, or blame. Rarely do these responses put us in a resourceful state. A smile lessens the bite of the moment and creates a better place from which to communicate. A smile sets up a positive chain reaction in our emotions and our bodies.*

🐾 *Dogs generally assume that events are happy and that people are good until proven otherwise. This invites a positive response. Smiling people also invite positive responses. Think of it as making deposits in the Bank of the Universe.*

🐾 *If you've ever awoken to a dog snuggled next to you, you know what it is to start your day with a smile. What other things make you smile—music, a photograph, a loved one's voice? Give yourself those things frequently! Notice what you attract when you're smiling more.*

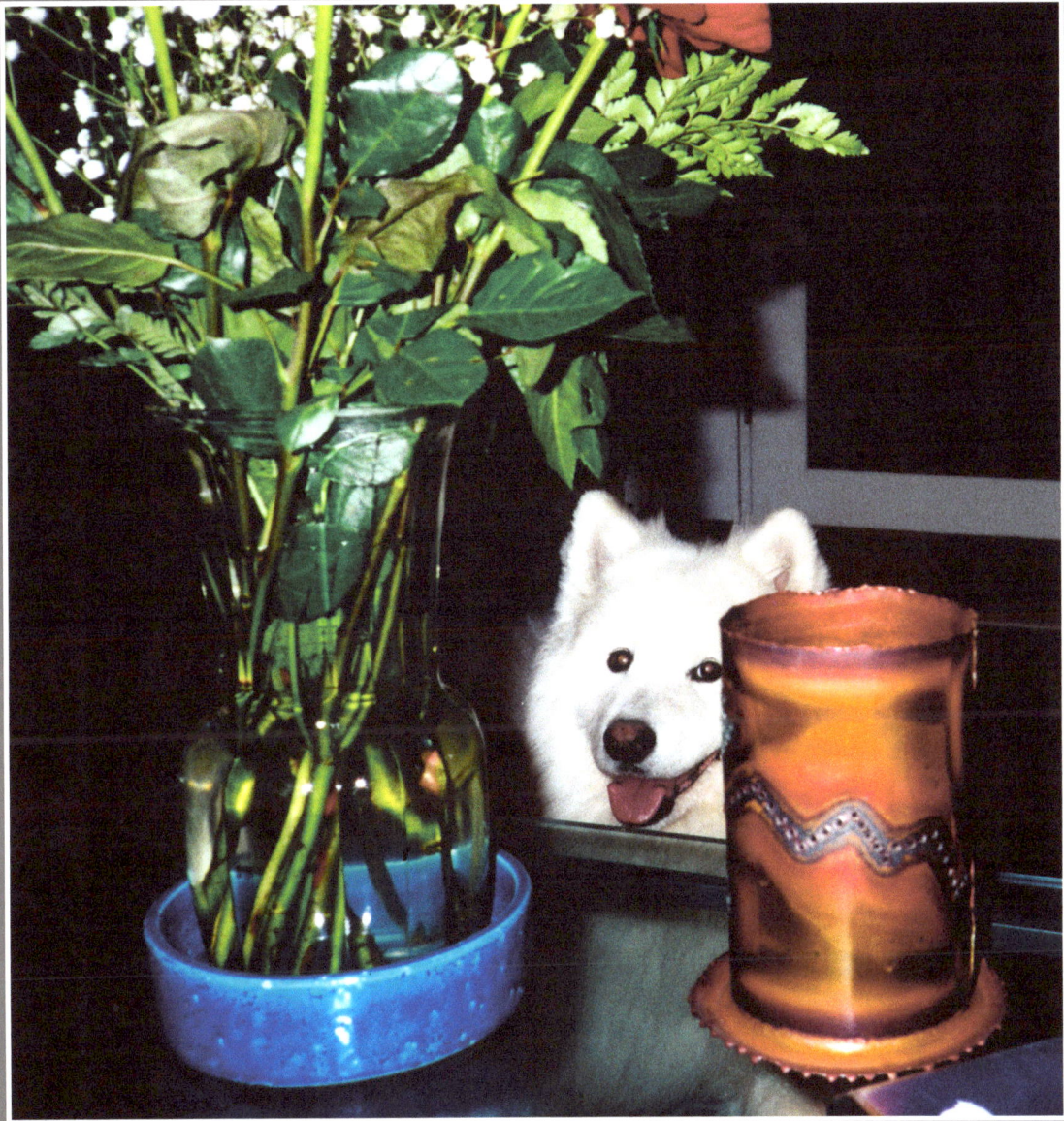

Good things come your way when you smile.

A WINNING SMILE

Getting Older

When you're just a young pup, life looks very different from when you're an old dog. When you're young, you have so much energy, and there's so much to discover. You learn that you don't have any manners, and that there's a lot more to learn, too. When you fall down, you practically bounce! It doesn't even hurt.

When you get older, falling down does hurt. But, with age you've learned a lot, so you get along pretty well in the world. All of a sudden some of your friends aren't around anymore, because they've passed on. It can be lonely sometimes. I used to jump up in a heartbeat, for any reason, and for no reason! I struggle a bit now—I have arthritis in my hips, and my knee surgery a couple of years ago says, "Hello Magellan!" on a regular basis. But I make do.

We older folks have a lot to offer. We have wisdom, gentleness, and compassion. We can teach what we know to young ones, so that they don't have to learn some things the hard way, like we did. We can appreciate being alive every day, and the small things, such as a good meal or a hug. We can enjoy watching youngsters run around like crazy, like we used to do, and rediscovery is a joy.

It's not easy getting older! It takes courage and heart. Remember that, little ones! Hug us and love us. Appreciate us.

THOUGHTFUL PAWS

🐾 *Dogs are really stoic. Despite pain and despite age, they always have a happy outlook. They look for what's right, not what's wrong. There has to be a correlation there.*

🐾 *Old dogs have very special energy. They teach younger dogs the ropes, and they know how to get along in the world. Elderly humans have special energy, too. Sometimes we have to learn how to tap that energy, and sometimes we just have to make some time and listen.*

🐾 *Every old dog was once an adorable puppy. That puppy is still in there, if you look. The same is true for elderly human beings— there is still a child, a vibrant youth, and an adult in their prime in there. Outward appearances can disguise these truths.*

Growing older gracefully takes courage and heart.

Love is Not a Tidy Thing

There are lots of ways to show your love. Kisses, for instance. Kisses can be neat little pecks or big, wet, and sloppy—that's the way I like 'em. Getting petted and cuddled by my family and friends is great, but they have to be willing to get covered with white hair. Hey, it's not a bad thing—I'm covered in white hair all the time.

You can show your love just by being with somebody when they're not feeling well. Sure, they're more fun when they're running around, and some unattractive things can go on during illness, like throwing up, but there's something special about "being there" for someone who's not feeling well. You can just tell how much they appreciate your comfort.

Ginger had two knee surgeries in one year. She had to stay in bed quite a bit, and couldn't take Magellan and me for our daily walks for over a month. Life wasn't as active as I generally like it. Magellan and I were right there for Ginger, though. We hung out by the bed or the sofa, and let her know that we were OK with it. More person for us!

It's easy to love someone when things are going great. But when they're in a bad mood, or do something wrong, that's when it really counts. I don't take bad moods personally. I know that it's something up with them, and I just be myself and give 'em a big, wet, sloppy kiss and cover them with white hair. It works out just fine!

THOUGHTFUL PAWS

❧ *God made puppies incredibly cute so that their humans would forgive them when they chew a shoe or eat the car's cruise control. Puppy mischief comes in the same package as puppy love! Our relationship with dogs is still one of the best deals ever.*

❧ *Dogs blissfully accept all of their humans' flaws: messiness, tardiness, temper—everything. Never do they judge. Imagine if people could accept each other that way. We could start with accepting our dogs' canine behaviors, hair on the sofa and even a little slobber.*

❧ *Loyalty is a beloved characteristic of dogs. They stick by you, no matter what. Our part of the bargain is to stick by our dogs when they are sick and when they grow old. Dogs model loyalty in ways that can inspire us in how we treat fellow humans, too.*

Tasja ever so gently takes a cookie offering.

Be An Optimist

Dogs are optimists. Do you ever see a dog thinking, "Oh, they won't give me a bite of *that* yummy tidbit!" No. We think, "Some of that delicious stuff is bound to come my way, any minute!" I am quite convinced (you've heard of manifestation, no doubt) that if I concentrate hard enough on the loaf of bread on the counter, it will eventually come down to me. Self-help may have to be invoked if it doesn't, of course. I am a primo Counter Surfer.

I just can't see the point in not being an optimist. Even when things don't work out just the way I'd hoped, I'm really happy right up until that point. And I'm resilient. When I'm told "No," I wait about ten seconds, then ask, "How 'bout now?" Again. 10-9-8-7-6-5-4-3-2-1… "How 'bout now?" "No right now" does not necessarily mean "no forever." Think about all the happiness that I would miss if I did not believe that good things were always about to come my way!

I don't know what's around the corner, but I feel confident that it will be good. If it isn't, I am confident that it will get better. Dread is not something I experience very often. Maybe when I see the toenail clippers come out—who doesn't experience dread then? But even then, I am optimistic that it will be over soon.

And you know what? Optimism is contagious! Sometimes, because I am so hopeful that I will get a cookie, and ask for one, the idea catches on and I get cookies! HAH! Just like in the movie, "The Secret." Well, the Secret's been out for a long time with me!

THOUGHTFUL PAWS

🐾 *Dogs are natural optimists. They are also generally happy. Think there's a correlation? Are you more of an optimist, or a pessimist? What shift would have to happen for you to feel more optimistic?*

🐾 *When confronted with a setback or an obstacle, is your first inclination to turn away and give up, or to think, "Hmm, how else might this happen?"*

🐾 *Optimism is contagious. Pessimism can be, too. What do you want to spread?*

Magellan using the power of suggestion, hoping for a walk.

Snooze Views

Life's too short to get all worked up. A good snooze is often just what's needed. Sometimes I get a little anxious if I'm left behind when Ginger leaves, or if Magellan won't leave me alone (you know how boys can be). But if I take a nice nap, things generally sort themselves out.

I'm an expert Power Napper. Here are some of my best tips:

1. Find a spot in the sun—there's nothing like sleeping in the sunshine!
2. Don't go to sleep mad—you want to have sweet dreams, not nightmares.
3. Pick the best possible spot for your snooze—like on the sofa or in the snow. Don't let anybody else tell you where the best spot is—their agenda might be different from yours.
4. If possible, sleep so that your tummy is in a position to be rubbed, should anyone feel the need to do so.

Some of the benefits of a good snooze are:

1. You wake up refreshed and in a good mood.
2. If something unpleasant was going on when you drifted off, maybe it's over!
3. When you're sick, naps help you heal and get better sooner.
4. Everyone's reminded of how sweet and innocent you look when you're asleep.
5. Your troubles just melt away… and anything is possible in your dreams. Sometimes I catch rabbits or eat a whole steak in my dreams! And cats—look out!

THOUGHTFUL PAWS

- *Difficulty falling asleep or sleeping well has become a widespread challenge for people. You almost never see a dog have trouble with either. What would it take for us to be willing to let our cares go, just long enough to rest well? The cares will be there when we wake. We'll be better equipped to address them if we can sleep well.*

- *Do you use dreams as a creative place? People sometimes forget that our subconscious is a tremendous resource, and that dreaming can be an alternative path to new solutions and ideas.*

- *Napping is easier for some people than for others. A snooze in the sun can be a wonderfully refreshing indulgence! Meditation is also a way to refresh without falling asleep, but still quieting the mind and utilizing the subconscious mind. When our lives are overwhelmingly busy is just when napping or meditation can yield the most benefit, yet require the most discipline to do.*

GINGER JENKS

If possible, sleep so that your tummy is in a position to be rubbed, should anyone feel the need to do so.

Sing Your Song

I enjoy singing. Ginger plays the trumpet, and it's especially fun to sing along with the trumpet! Mind you, I am gifted with a lovely singing voice. But even if I weren't, I think it would be important to sing anyway. There's something about vocalizing in a different way that is freeing, and fun.

Sometimes when we are traveling and in a hotel room, Ginger tells me, "Sssshhhhh!" when I sing. Imagine. I go along with the request out of courtesy, but it seems silly to me. One should always be able to sing when one is so moved.

I see and hear people singing in their cars, sometimes. I love car rides, don't you? But back to singing…. I wonder why people sing in their cars where no one can hear them. They look so happy and confident when they think no one can hear them. Why is that? But I can hear them, of course, with my SuperSamoyed hearing. They all make me smile, for one reason or another. You should hear them!

Here's the deal. I think there are literally billions of songs by people that are going unsung. That's a lot of music missing in the world. Dogs are easy to read—we tell the truth. We sing when we have a song. We don't worry about how we sound, or how we look. I sing because there is a song in my heart, and it simply must be sung.

THOUGHTFUL PAWS

🐾 *Seriously, how often do you let yourself sing out loud, with everything you've got? Try it daily for a week. Find a safe place, if you need to.*

🐾 *What song is in your heart that has not yet been sung? Is it worth finding the time, and the courage, to express that "song"? If not now, when?*

🐾 *Does part of your authentic self get stifled, for fear of how you think others will view the way you sound, or the way you look? How great would it feel to be more of yourself, more of the time?*

Singing the National Anthem to kick off a national dog show!

SING YOUR SONG

I'm Here Today

My human, Ginger, is very sad today. Bad news bites. My doctor said I have cancer, and that I'm going to die soon. About six months ago I started having to have shots twice a day for something called "diabetes." I take a whole bunch of pills every day. It's not such a bad thing, though, because Ginger mixes them up with delicious food and I just chow 'em right down.

I'm here today. That's what I know. I've felt better before, but there's still lots of good things about today. Hugs from Ginger. Yummy food. Kisses from Magellan. A walk in the Colorado sunshine. Basking out on the front deck. Interesting new scents to sniff. My leg hurts a bit and I'm tired, but I'm OK. I'm 12 now, and that's getting up there for a dog.

Tonight, Ginger and Magellan lay beside me and Ginger told us stories about all the wonderful times we've had together over the last twelve years. I'd forgotten some of that fun stuff! I'm glad I've helped to make Ginger and Magellan's lives happy. They do the same for me! We all drifted off to sleep cuddled up like that. Nice. If there was ever a better evening, I don't know it. It was like camping in the living room. I love camping, don't you?

THOUGHTFUL PAWS

- *When bad news bites, how well do you do at keeping it in perspective? Are you able to still be yourself?*

- *Resilience is a quality worth cultivating! When a dog has a setback, they are quick to bounce back, and expect the best. This serves them well in living happier, healthier lives. How quickly do you bounce back?*

- *Sometimes, despite bad news on the horizon, the Present is still perfect. Don't waste beautiful moments now in angst over what may be in the future.*

Magellan in mountain wildflowers atop Yankee Boy Basin, Ouray, CO.

I'M HERE TODAY

All Dogs Go to Heaven

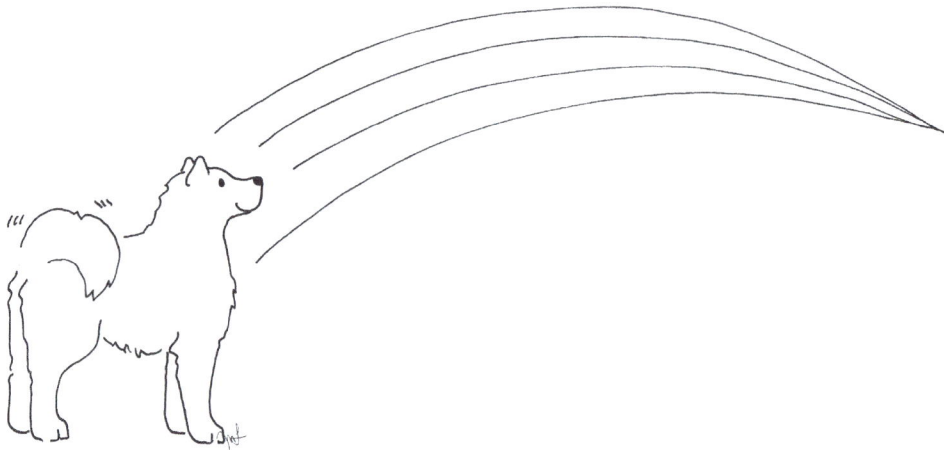

All dogs go to heaven, they say. Can heaven be here with my friends and family? That's where I want to be. Ginger keeps asking me, "Is it Time?" Gosh, I don't know. I'm relying on her for that. She's promised to keep me safe and happy. I know she'll keep her promise. My promise is just to let her know if I'm hurting. I am.

We've had lots of good times over the past two months. It's been a special time for me. It's good to be Queen. Car rides, walks, cheeseburgers from McDonald's, the Beggar's Ball.... Hey, the food gets really good when you're dying!

Becky, my doctor, is at the door. Ginger's crying. It must be Time. It's OK, Ginger. Just hold me and tell me again that you love me. My spirit will always be with you, and yours with me. Thank you for setting my body free. I'll see you in heaven, over the Rainbow Bridge. Bring cookies, OK?

THOUGHTFUL PAWS

* *A sacred responsibility we owe our dogs is to let them go when it is Time—when they are suffering without prospect of relief. It's unbearably painful for the human, yet peaceful for the dog. Pain and peace can co-exist within us.*

* *When it is Time? When the prognosis is a brief life expectancy, perhaps the words of Tasja's vet are a gift: "Today is not too soon, and tomorrow is not too late."*

* *When our time with a loved one is ending, everyday concerns fall away. We experience our relationship as fully as possible. But in truth, our time together is always limited, and we never know when it will end. If we brought that heightened consciousness to our relationships now, how much richer would our experience be?*

JIM SALDON

Tasja enjoying a blissful moment of peace and joy.

Grief Used to be Joy

TASJA

Grief is a very powerful thing.

When I lost my best friend Tasja, I suddenly got old. I was old all along, but I didn't know it, because my love for her kept me young. When she died, all of a sudden my back legs were sore all the time, my tummy hurt and I just kind of felt tired every day.

I miss her all the time. She was so great! For a while, I kept thinking maybe she'd come back, even though I got to say goodbye to her when she left. Now I know that she's really gone, and I'm very sad.

At first after Tasja died, I didn't feel like living any more either. But it's getting a little better, now that a few months have passed. A new little Samoyed friend came to join our family. His name is Rory. He kind of makes me crazy, but I kind of like him, too. He makes me laugh again. Puppies are like that. Tasja was a great puppy. I harassed her a lot when she was little. Maybe that's why Rory is harassing me so much—what goes around, comes around! No fair. I think Rory is a Karma puppy.

I'll never forget Tasja. Grief is a very powerful thing. I guess it hurts so much because it used to be joy. Ginger says that a human named Kahlil Gibran said, "When you are sorrowful look again your heart, and you shall see that in truth you are weeping for that which has been your delight." That sounds right to me.

THOUGHTFUL PAWS

* *People who think that dogs don't experience emotion would change their minds if they had witnessed Magellan's obvious grief over Tasja's death. Grief is the flip side of joy, and to deny our dogs respect for their emotions is to do them a serious disservice. Imagine someone saying to you, "Oh, you don't really feel that."*

* *Platitudes generally become platitudes because there is some truth in them. There is truth in the platitude about time helping to heal grief. It can be so sharp and deep when fresh. Believing that it will ever feel differently requires courage. Even witnessing the grief of someone close to you requires courage—to simply be there for that someone.*

* *Does love disappear when the loved one disappears?*

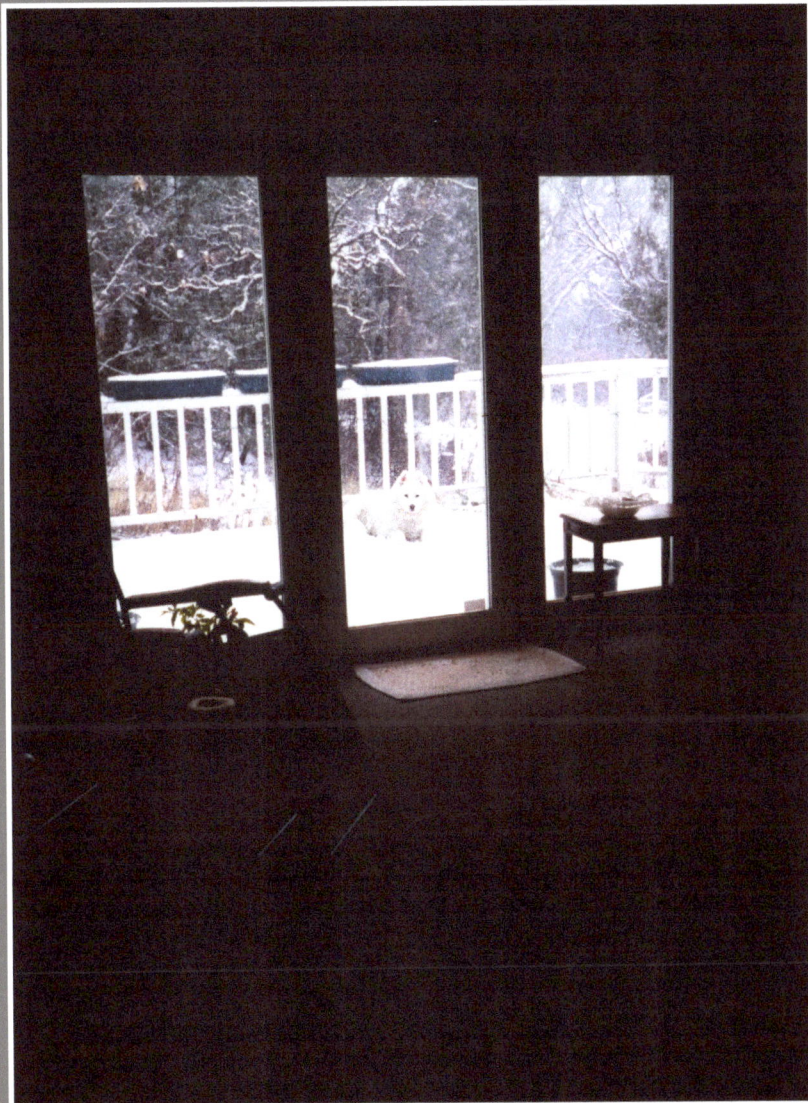

GINGER JENKS

Tasja loved to rest in the snow, especially in her later years.

Healing and Joy

When you lose somebody you love, like I lost Tasja, you feel like your heart is breaking. You're not even sure you want to go on, even though you still have good things in your life, like I have my human, Ginger. Loss hurts, and you have to find ways to heal.

We did some cool things to help us heal. We read stories like this, and watched Tasja on a videotape—she was so **beautiful!** Ginger also made a Memory Garden in our front yard, in honor of Tasja. I helped dig it! I'm an excellent digger. There are lots of pink and white flowers, even some roses called "Climbing the Pearly Gates." I like that. There are also two sets of wind chimes hanging from a tree branch, that our friends Dianne and Marcy gave us. Every morning, when we go for our walk, Ginger rings the chimes, and we say, "Hi Tasja! We love you and remember you!" And I think she knows this, and I know she still loves us, too.

Rory, my new adopted puppy brother, isn't the same as Tasja, but it's helped to have the company. And he's fun! I'm his hero. Please. He was born ten days after Tasja died, and I think he's got some of her spirit in him—I see it sometimes. Like when he takes my rawhide chewy away from me, or when he lies next to me and puts his head on my paw. It's good to know that life goes on, and that there is still joy!

THOUGHTFUL PAWS

🐾 *After a loss, there can be a conflict between feeling sad and starting to feel better, even to laugh. Feeling joy again does not diminish the significance of the loss. We are not made to stay sad forever.*

🐾 *After losing a beloved dog, some folks say, "I'll never get another dog. I can't go through this kind of pain again." Or, "I don't want to try and replace her." New life is not about "replacing"—it is about honoring the wonderful feelings you had for the one who is gone, and risking your heart in the hopes of experiencing such love again.*

🐾 *Rituals help. Don't be shy about doing rituals to help you heal, for any kind of loss. Logic isn't particularly useful in healing grief. But rituals can connect the dots in different ways that make sense to your subconscious, as well as your heart.*

Rory and Magellan by Tasja's Memory Garden.

HEALING AND JOY

Little Ones

This new puppy, Rory, is something. I like him best when he's sleeping. It's nice to have the company, but he just won't leave me alone! He jumps on me, nips at my paws, and follows me everywhere. He wants to be with me every minute, and do everything I do.

Ginger says I should be nice to him, and teach him stuff. I would, but I'll tell you, puppies are just plain silly. He can hardly sit still long enough for me to teach him anything. Today he was running in circles, chasing his tail. He finally caught it, and fell over—right into the water bowl! You should have seen the look on his face.

Rory came from a top breeder in Denver. She said Rory can grow up to be a Champion show dog, and that his ancestors are all Champions. Hmmph. *I* could have been a contender....

We have a wading pool. It's nice to cool your feet off in it on summer days. This Rory puppy has a majorly Big Time in it. He jumps in it from a dead run, and the water goes everywhere. And then he digs in it, and the water goes everywhere some more. Honestly, he *digs* in it! Surely I couldn't have been so ridiculous when I was a pup.

I watch out for him, even if he does annoy me sometimes. After all, there are bears outside, hot ovens inside, and he probably wouldn't last a day without me. I guess he's OK, after all. I like him best when he's sleeping, though.

THOUGHTFUL PAWS

- *Young beings test our patience. They also worry us. And they amaze us and make us laugh. They are a pain in the butt. All are true. Paradoxes are OK.*

- *How do you behave differently if you are a hero to someone? Does it make you strive to live up to the hero image, and be the best person you can be?*

- *Think back to when you were younger, and who you looked up to. Who are the people who made a difference in your life? What qualities in them do you admire? Do Little Ones experience those same qualities in you? Little Ones can help us to remember who we want to be. Dogs can help us to remember and discover those things as well.*

Rory the puppy with his hero, Magellan.

LITTLE ONES

SWEET TASJA DIED JUNE 5, 2001. I had to make the decision for her. When your pet friend is in too much pain, you have to be kind and help her to die. Tasja had as good a final two months as could be hoped for, given her disease. I still miss Tasja, but continue to be grateful for having known her. Magellan grieved sorely for Tasja the first couple of months. Rory cheered him considerably. And Rory and Magellan both cheered me considerably. They brought love and joy to me every day, and a smile to everyone they met. Magellan died September 25, 2002, at almost 14 years of age. Rory's story continues, and he has a new Samoyed girlfriend—Imp! Rory and Imp are planning to write their own book.

Tasja at age 12 with her Favorite Human.

www.ingramcontent.com/pod-product-compliance
Lightning Source LLC
Chambersburg PA
CBHW040038120426
42742CB00046B/45